"Cry whenever you need to. Scream. Shout.
Lay on the floor. Sob in the shower.
Be Still. Run. Walk. Create. Live your truth.
Share without fear. Listen. Release your pain.
Breathe. Be courageous. Throw away the map.
Wander. Be real. Be Compassionate.
Read. Seek friendship. Be vulnerable.
Don't fear being broken."

Zoe Clark-Coates

"I am deeply connected to all that is nature. I rely on this space
to enhance my overall wellbeing. This space nurtures me and in
turn, I must reciprocate this relational dynamic. I need to tread
lightly, very lightly. It starts with me and you and him and her and
them. We all have a responsibility. The degree of responsibility
that the individual, the giant beasts of business and the
government have is debatable. But we all have a responsibility."

Robyn Hughes, Therapist, The Cavernoma Alliance

"We must now agree on a binding review mechanism under international law so that this century can credibly be called a century of decarbonisation."

Angela Merkel

"Wendy's writing is both insightful and sobering. Putting the slow death of our beautiful planet into a grief and bereavement framework makes interesting and thought-provoking reading. There seemed to be an optimistic period during the covid pandemic, but as time has gone on, this has appeared less hopeful. The scale and the danger of the climate crisis still seems to challenge our thinking. Whilst we are still able to buy £30 flights to the sun, our own habits of mind, along with the fossil fuel industry, are something we must urgently overcome."

Rachel Walker, Cruse Bereavement Support

Mother is Dying
A societal and trauma analysis into climate change and what you can do about it

By

Wendy Wren

AUSTIN MACAULEY PUBLISHERS™
LONDON • CAMBRIDGE • NEW YORK • SHARJAH

ISBN 9781398489776 (Paperback)
ISBN 9781398489783 (ePub e-book)

www.austinmacauley.com

First Published 2022
Austin Macauley Publishers Ltd
1 Canada Square
Canary Wharf
London E14 5AA

"There is a pleasure in the pathless woods,
There is a rapture on the lonely shore,
There is Society, where none intrudes,
By the deep sea and music in its roar:
I love not man the less but nature more."

Lord Byron

———————

Dedicated to
the human energy
that burns between us

———————

---

*"The natural world is in
crisis because of us."*
Sir David Attenborough

Foreword

Wendy's book is no understatement. It is a book that every cognitive human being should read. Wendy captures every eco and emotional detail, from the current eco facts to what lays, practically and emotionally, ahead of us.

When it comes to choices about the environment and diet, people hear so much about sadness and negativity, that they crave happy stories and as a result, 'hide their heads in the sand'. This enables their consciousness and unconsciousness to think it's somebody else's job to sort out.

This book captures a rising eco and more emotionally aware movement. It can be anything, but something, choosing to become vegan or plant based, going to refillable shops, buying an e-car, changing our homes, shopping differently, lobbying peacefully and so on.

Wendy captures an important message; that everyone needs to take on some eco-responsibility, and that by working together, we can all, make a practical and emotional difference, to this world.

From a psychological perspective, Wendy identifies, that people connect with others, via social media and in person, with those, similar to themselves. As a result, our thoughts and ways of thinking can condition others to have stronger views. This is because every link we follow emphasises our personal way of living which can lead to stronger inflexible ideas, being reinforced, by others, with the same attitude.

Wendy explores, in various parts of the book, how love and hate, can become polarised opposites. She explores how individuals frequently only get acceptance from those that are ready to accept the morals and choices of a group or individual. Wendy explores this dichotomy & denial on how individuals do not like, act or follow, because they don't want to hear something (eco) or are not ready to face impending reality. As a result, people are reluctant to engage with material and lifestyles they cannot face. Subsequently, they will not receive more information or link to those friendship groups.

Wendy captures how people attach onto threads that are positive and often non-political, so that their lives can be lived in a more manageable, superficial, funny, light-hearted, meaningful and doable way. The problem is that this is not sustainable.

There often needs to be a crisis situation before people alter their behaviour. Covid 19 has changed some people's behaviour but much more, at every societal level, needs to be done.

Wendy's book is ultimately a book of hope. It covers what needs to be done and what will happen if we do not act. Her bereavement analysis and predictions around future behaviours are pretty sobering.

Certainly, we need to move from a Me to a Us culture. Our future, and that of our children, depends upon Us.

Wendy paves the way for how emotionally re-connecting and making changes to our lifestyle can really change our place and experience in this world. She reflects on a world which can be nourishing and healthy. I commend her book to you and I hope that you seek out the positive personal changes that she clearly sets out.

Susan Nold
Vegan

———————

"It is our collective and individual responsibility... to preserve and tend to the world in which we all live."

Dalai Lama

———————

Many a vegan has said to me, "You cannot be properly eco-friendly unless you give up all meat." If only it was that simple! What we don't need is more preaching. To be honest, we are virtually gagging on our celery over that argument. But the vegans do have a point and they are at least taking the time to think and take stock. So, let's take a look at the whole story, from climate change and global warming, to gaining insight and potentially changing our own, and societal, behaviour.

The feeling I have, at the moment, frankly, is a feeling of detachment. Global warming is something that somebody else is going to sort out for me. I do not wish to be executor of the will or have power of attorney for Mother Earth. But perhaps we all have to take on this role?

I keep being told what I need to do – indeed, what I *must* do, again and again. The subject of climate change has become, dare I say it, boring.

Until the subject is approached in an appropriate and relatable way, I will continue to think that it is out of my reach and somebody else's responsibility.

The subject we need to emotionally engage with is the fact that *Mother Earth is dying*. The only way this will happen is if we connect with the subject, on an emotional, personal and societal level.

The true essence of global warming and climate change is indeed, dramatically and devastatingly that: our Mother is honestly, slowly, dying. Her lungs are full of heat, smog, confusion and congestion. Her heart is slow, painful and aching. Her legs and feet are now getting increasingly swollen and rather wobbly.

Is it no wonder that we push the subject of Mother dying to the back of our minds? How can we even begin to get our heads around the fact that we may all go first? We may all die tragically, destructively, politically or quietly. We may die just before Mother does, such is our sense of detachment, denial and internal disorder.

Moreover, the increased heat temperatures, brought about by global warming, will have a direct impact and correlation with our cellular health. As a result, chronic health conditions will be both activated and exacerbated. Consequently, remaining healthy, and taking individual responsibility, will no longer be a lifestyle choice but also a pre-requisite to physical and emotional survival. It will also be necessary, to make these health adjustments, if our health establishments, are not to be over burdened. Significantly, individual responsibility is directly linked to community responsibility, governmental investment, having enough good people 'for the job' and new, potentially kinder, global value systems.

In this book, I take a psychodynamic and bereavement perspective in order to engage the reader in a relatable way. I set out the facts and potential consequences of global warming and climate change. I further discuss the solutions, on the macro and micro level, which are urgently needed.

Centrally, I use the analysis of trauma, bereavement and loss, so that we can understand, more deeply and more confluently, what climate change means and why we may choose to engage and act. I also explore how bereavement theory can be applied to planet degeneration.

Introduction

We are no longer in the 1950s, sometimes considered an era of division. For the most part, we are now educationally and socially engaged with our fellow human beings. To live confluently, with a shared and emotional vision, we need to share and feel how our future may look. This is essentially what it is, first and foremost, to be *human*(e). As we learn to respect each other, we learn to respect the emotional and physical space around us. Despite a minority who continue to practice discrimination, most of us have evolved into more diverse, respectful, tolerant and sensitive human beings. We perhaps now need to focus on our similarities, as much as our differences.

How does the very design of many societies align alongside our new norms? How do we combine capitalism with equality, humanity and progress? How do we become 'jointly responsive' on so many physical and emotional levels? What is going on here? It is the subject of our time: Mother Earth is dying...

At the end of the book, you can make your own choice, on behalf of the planet – what will *you* do to help? What change will you support, or continue to support, in your communities? And what pressure will you put upon others to bring about change?

How can we think about becoming more emotionally connected human beings? The loss of planet earth will either bring us together or divide us. The power of emotional good health and good community engagement lies within us all. We are all, indeed, citizens of the world.

———————

"No matter what people tell you,
words and ideas change the world."

Dead Poets Society

———————

The purpose of this chapter is to provide a high-level summary on global warming, human impact and the governmental, local and individual action required to combat it. It provides a 'backdrop' to the topic of analysing the contextual experience and current and future emotional and practical impact of climate change, which we cover later on. It is at the end of the book that identification, connection and links between the different chapters should occur.

Introductory Statement.

The United Nations (UN) set out a 2020 deadline to save nature, but not a single target was met.

We are at a point where it is too warm already to stop the melting of the permafrost. More gases will be released to create more heat, which will in turn warm up the planet even more. Subsequently, more permafrost will melt more ice sheets and due to the lack of ice sheets remaining to reflect the sunlight, our planet will absorb more heat from the sun's energy. As a result, oceans will become significantly warmer and sea levels will rise further. We will experience an increase in hurricanes and typhoons, and coastal cities will become flooded, due to the rise in sea levels. The rate of melting we are experiencing today already exceeds anything Greenland has experienced in the last 12,000 years.

Greenhouse gas emissions link directly to energy activity. Carbon dioxide is just one of several gases which is causing the '*greenhouse effect*', responsible for 76% of global warming. Next is methane at 16% and nitrogen oxide at 6%, both of which are mainly emitted during agricultural and industrial processes (Nature Journal 2020).

The world currently produces about 33 gigatons of carbon dioxide each year and this is increasing daily. Generally speaking, developed and developing countries are producing far more pollution problems than poorer countries. However, the impact of this man-made pollution is non-discriminatory in terms of who it effects.

To clarify, global warming refers to the earth's rising surface temperature, while climate change includes the actual warming and the side effects of warming. Subsequently, global warming is one symptom of the much larger problem of human-caused climate change. Other areas of global climate misuse are explored later in the book.

I asked my 12-year-old to write down what climate change meant to her generation. Whilst she does not represent every 12-year old's voice, or angle, here is what she said, in her own words:

"I used to believe it provided people with jobs; I believed fast fashion provided people with cheap clothing, which may not be affordable to some normally. After watching a documentary entitled 'Fashion's Dirty Secrets', it gave me an insight into what fashion really is. I wholeheartedly believe that fashion has caused detrimental impacts to our home and the environment around us. The evidence for this has been around us *this whole time*. For example, the clothing industry is the second worst polluter in the world, after oil. We have stolen time before and it is now *out of our hands*. We are struggling to deal with the impact as 100 billion garments are thrown away every year. Why is this, you may be wondering... Well, it all starts with where a lot of cotton is produced, in Kazakhstan. The Aral Sea was the biggest inland sea mass and it now symbolises the effects of cotton trading. Shrinking constantly since 1977, the Aral Sea, which used to be the size of Ireland, is causing extreme weather changes, with temperatures now reaching up to 35 degrees. The eco-system has died, killing the fishing industry with it. Sandstorms, filled with chemicals from cotton farms, have created many health issues. All this for *fashion* so that people can purchase more clothes than they need, while it is 'on trend' and extremely desirable. Nearly 50 years' worth of drinking water for people's everyday clothes shopping. Why are we using (and wasting) so much water to manufacture clothes when people cannot afford food and water to wash for one day, let alone 49 years? You cannot even talk to the retailers about the damage they are causing.

Moreover, it is a constant downward spiral as we see the environmental impacts of over 400 factories, depositing plastic and chemicals, which is poisonous to the environment and the people living there. It is their vital source of water and it is completely untreated, causing many health problems to the local people and children. I would just like to say that people's, animals' and nature's health and lives depend on better environmental conditions, which are currently disastrous because of YOU!"

This is an interesting reflection of what my 12-year-old has learnt with the educational focus being fashioned-centred. She captures very well the multi-model layers of human impact on the environment, both sociologically, personally, collectively, geographically and commercially.

World Wildlife Fund's 'One Planet Perspective' outlines how we need to make better choices for managing, using and sharing our natural resources, within Mother Earth's limits. This would ensure food, water and energy security for all.

It requires that we:

Preserve natural capital – Restore damaged ecosystems, halt the loss of priority habitats and significantly expand protected areas.

Produce better – Reduce inputs and waste, manage resources sustainably and sale-up renewable energy production.

Consume more wisely – Through low-footprint lifestyles, sustainable energy use and healthier food consumption patterns.

Redirect financial flows – Value nature, account for environmental and social costs, support and reward conservation, sustainable resource management and innovation.

Have equitable resource governance – Share available resources, make fair and ecologically informed choices and measure success beyond financial gain.

Energy is integral to modern life because it underpins everything we do, from cooking, heating our homes, manufacturing metals, transporting goods and travelling to work, to name just a few. This 'progression' has been underpinned by major social transformations during The Industrial Revolution, a time where human development and progress somewhat side-lined religion in mainstream consciousness. This is not to say it replaced religion, but it certainly underpinned what we did and how we started to *think and live*. It underscored not just social norms but social values too. Prosperity, invention and 'successes' have frequently been underpinned by the use of coal, oil and gas.

The use of technology is therefore multi-model; it is not just a matter of doing things differently. It is about living differently, thinking differently, appreciating things differently and valuing life over possessions. No technology is necessarily 'pure'. It is sometimes just about doing things in a better way, being 'good enough', more measured and thoughtful.

There is a goal of 'net-zero per person target' being bandied about, with different time dimensions and agendas. In simple terms, people must *give* back as much as they *take*, from the environment.

In the UK, the growth of offshore wind turbines and their cost competitiveness against fossil fuels is credited with spurring a substantial decline in carbon emissions for electricity generation over the past decade, also making the biggest contribution to the UK's overall carbon reduction. In 2019, 20% of the UK's electricity was generated by wind and, as we moved into 2020, the first quarter's figures showed a staggering 30%. The current trend in offshore wind energy is for turbines to get even bigger and, with more areas of the sea bed being offered up for development all the time, the stage is set for a super-growth in this sector. Globally, wind capacity is expected to go up by an incredible 112% over the next decade, growing from 29GW capacity now to well over 234GW by 2030. The UK government recently announced a goal to "quadruple current offshore wind capacity of 10 GW to a staggering 40GW, by 2030" (*The Future of Energy*: page 36).

Solar energy also has the potential to be expanded. Whilst not perfect and requiring long-term replacement, it is a step in the right direction and has seen a tenfold increase. More creative options have seen some governments committing to incorporating solar panel into rooftop tiles. Moreover, older styles of building, such as mud and thatched roofs, also provide non-toxic alternatives. The insulation of roof space is an established option, which serves to reduce heat loss and keep homes cosier and costing less to heat. Additionally, if people buy less 'rubbish', they can create more storage space in their lofts!

Wood is another product widely used in around 10% of global energy production and in other ways too. Whether it is used for heating or furnishing, wood consumption needs to be re-considered. The 'buy-cheap' manufacture of furniture requires a re-evaluation on how we buy and how we *value* our own homes. The degeneration of furniture is a natural process and it should be upcycled – also known as 'creative reuse'. The 'buy then throw away' culture does need to change if we are to use less wood. The replenishment of trees cannot keep up with the increased levels of deforestation. Change and action is required regarding re-planting projects. These issues are complex, both politically and locally. In terms of market forces, other local trade, of the same value, needs to be made available, if this increase is going to be reversed. It is estimated that the Amazon rainforest only has 10 sustainable years remaining, on its current trajectory. Additionally, housing and urbanisation has had a huge impact on green spaces and wildlife. The requirement to restore some of these areas to their natural habitat is now urgent.

Despite a minority focus on newer technologies, fossil fuel currently still steals 78% of global energy production. The fact that it is running out and becoming more expensive is largely ignored. Gas central heating is still used widely despite people not setting timers to turn temperatures down and its link to ill-health. Air-source heating provides a greener and more comfortable form of heating. Many new houses are being installed with heating systems to be greener and more progressive. Additionally, long-term, they are already cheaper to run. With the UK's heating system averaging a D-grade classification, we could do a lot better! This doesn't just depend on government grants; it also depends on people choosing to spend their money differently and more wisely.

With that said, the 'best' and cheapest current heating option is an 'air to air' pump. This is slightly different to the 'ground to air source' pump version, currently supported by the U.K. government. At approximately £1,250 rather than £5-6,000, in terms of personal cost, the 'air to air' is preferable and will reduce the use of your electricity bills by 80 to 90%. Mathematically, it is not difficult to calculate an 'air to air' investment as a 'good' ecological and financial option.

In the future, Artificial Intelligence (AI) and 'smart' controls can start to make a lot of eco-decisions for us. Just as you can select the type of route you want to take on a satellite navigation system, a smart system links together consumption, local generation and supply data, to provide the optimum outcome, based on consumer wishes / eco needs. *The Future of Energy* states, "Perhaps the most enticing technology for decarbonisation is the idea of carbon capture and storage. The idea is to capture carbon dioxide at the point of release (burning in power stations or industrial processes, for example) and instead of sending it into the atmosphere, pump it deep underground and store it under pressure. This is a proven technology and could enable even the dirtiest of fossil fuels (like coal) to have a future. However, the costs of the process have, to date, made carbon capture and storage an enticing and yet unfulfilled technology", (Page 44).

Synthetic fuels could also provide new options for decarbonisation. This will require a shift away from the current thinking that 'synthetic is bad'.

Trucks, aviation and marine transport also contribute a devastating impact on global warming. The negative effects of air travel are well-covered in the media. This is sometimes due to their association with fame, over-indulgence and greed. However, one of the biggest polluters of our planet is mass marine transportation. Underpinning these huge cargo vehicles and multi-million-pound industries are companies such as Amazon and of course, the general consumer. The current shortage of lorry drivers in many developed countries is not necessarily a bad thing for planet earth, nor was the reduction of smog during the worldwide Covid-19 lockdowns.

The Future of Energy (2021) states that, to expand e-fuels, you need plenty of pure hydrogen and carbon monoxide. Carbon monoxide is made by passing carbon dioxide through the novelle 'reverse water gas shift'. This technique uses electricity to split up the carbon dioxide molecules, found in burning methane, coal and also biomass. The benefit of using carbon dioxide, produced during combustion, is that rather than being released into the atmosphere, it can be recycled.

Nuclear energy and ammonia are also areas currently being explored by scientists. However, both require a shift in human consciousness. This is because nuclear energy is often associated with bombs, leaks, mass demise and dare I say, death. Even the chemical process of splitting the nucleus of atoms comes with health and safety implications and inevitably, local apprehension and concern. Scientists are currently looking into 'fusion', with the underlying goal to produce energy which has limited waste and reduced risks. If the impact of the global pandemic leads to more localised living, then smaller constructed nuclear technology provides newer and greener solutions.

Biomass as a renewable energy source is problematic as it is generated from burning wood, plants and other organic matter. However, ideas around biogas are an exciting prospect, to potentially harness local power effectively. It's produced when organic matter, such as food or animal waste, is broken down by micro-organisms in the absence of oxygen, in a process called anaerobic digestion. For this to take place, the waste material needs to be enclosed in an environment where there is no oxygen.

Generating electricity from capturing the coastal tides also has the potential to deliver one-fifth of global energy demand. Although this method would have a local impact, the lure of zero-carbon energy is enormous.

The progression of technology around electric vehicles is exciting. Many countries are expanding their hook-up ability, with new houses being required to provide 'hosting stations'. Some areas have already seen neighbourhoods share this type of technology. The general population in developed countries have seen an emotional value shift to electric cars. However, ensuring an effective power source, the look and the hook-up is essential to this development. The real time to re-charge needs to be shortened if it is to be fully embraced. However, as politicians and other leaders turn to electric, this provides effective role modelling for adult individuals in society. As costs around buying and running motor cars rise, there has also been a shift away from some young people using or buying them, thus not always immediately signing up to the status symbolism of a car. These decisions are also effected by the general rising cost of living and housing. Massive investment and support of e-cars is essential if the market is to expand further. A compulsory reduction on the number of cars per household is also an option for governments to consider.

We are also seeing an increase in rentals, with many people seeing taxi or Uber journeys as an alternative to owning and running a car. Effective train travel, if delivered environmentally, could also be developed further. Domestic air travel is likely to remain reduced, due to the increase in home working, the desire for people not to wear masks for elongated periods and the bad press that multiple leisure journeys are receiving. Going on holiday five times a year is most definitely out of fashion these days! The student 'gap year' is also being experienced in new, more local ways.

Amazon and other organisations have 'got in' on the clothes rental demand, though Amazon continues to come under attack by the sheer fact that it needs to manoeuvre its products. In some respects, Amazon has made small attempts to become a little more eco-friendly. Clearly, investing in space travel was not one of their finer moments! Energy from space is another potential source of energy. However, there are problems not just with obtaining it, but the risks from terrorist attacks too.

In additional to global warming, we have some further problems that require multi-model address. For example, we need to drastically revisit how land is used for livestock and its consequential balance with nature and the preservation of wildlife and fauna. We need to explore fishing styles and rights and understand how this is destroying our sea beds. We need to consider 'food mountains', from unused food waste, plastic in the oceans, garbage in our water and on our beaches. There is too much plastic and waste in our waters. Apart from beach cleans, it is essential that we embrace new creative ideas about how to clean the ocean and to stop pollution and dumping in it, or using it, in the first place. There is also the increased threat of fast-spreading algae in our oceans, which is also choking the lungs of Mother Earth.

We are currently experiencing a mass hunger-obesity paradox of over consumption versus starvation. Wealth over poverty and self-interest over inequality. There is a local push for recycling and e-cars, but we need to go much, much further, at the micro and macro-level.

The Earthshot Prize, conceived by Sir David Attenborough and HRH Prince William, also provides some creative and progressive global ideas and development. It focuses on the following five distinct areas:

1. **Restore nature**
2. **Fix climate temperature**
3. **Clean our air**
4. **Restore ocean production**
5. **Create a waste-free world**

This is an approach that makes us feel that we can 'achieve anything'; 'it's a decade of action' and 'there is no time to waste'.

The different prizes and categories help to spur on ingenious, creative and novel ways of addressing the challenge of global warming. Many solutions are multi-model and varied, often reflecting a local need. Expanding these potential solutions to the macro-level, which has been done in some areas, is an exciting area for scientists, organisations and individuals. Moreover, scientists are battling away to improve the current status quo and also find new, exciting and innovative ideas for eco-implementation.

In a 2019 poll, Frank Luntz found that 75% of Americans wanted government intervention in order to limit carbon emissions. However, concerns were expressed that voters' apprehensions were not being adequately addressed. As in other developed and developing countries, we face the challenge of trying to fundamentally alter capitalism. In poorer countries, there is also a knock-on effect of some countries having disproportionately less impact on global warming but being inadvertently more greatly affected by it. These countries' issues continue to reach the realm of the mainstream media and social platforms, yet there is still an absence of clear, SMART and reviewable approaches to address them.

Capitalism is defined as an economic and social system, which is based upon the private ownership of the means of production and their operation for profit. Central characteristics of capitalism include capital accumulation, competitive markets, a price system, private property, property rights, voluntary exchange and paid labour. Underpinning capitalism is the studying for a particular profession or the learning of a trade or craft. Usually, any distinct changes to capitalism are led by market forces. This is caused by over-demand resulting in less profit.

Historically, particularly during The Industrial Revolution, working choices were sociologically implemented and changed. In the modern world, it is unusual for people to alter their profession or trade. Consequently, capitalism underpins the life of many individuals in society. Contributions from paid work support some welfare states, which also perpetuates capitalism. Many individuals have mortgages or rent to pay, so are reliant on the continuation of their job, whether that job be eco-friendly or not. Many forms of employment, in their own right, may not significantly affect the planet, but the place of work, the getting to work and the thinking about work are all interconnected. As such, our social and psychological systems support the very foundations of capitalism. This indirectly effects the planet, without people necessarily consciously realising it. Where people do realise the impact of their 'carbon footprint', they are often at the economic mercy of continuing their way of living to simply survive. Moreover, in poorer countries, there may not be the gender freedom or work opportunities to even engage in capitalism. It's a gargantuan task to fully break down capitalism, in a way that Mother Earth requires. It not only changes how we live, but how we create our identities and our life purpose. Change is therefore as much an emotional transition as a physical one.

Marketing and social media are powerful tools to encourage change but as human beings, we need to be increasingly *smarter*. Can we not see through the 'cookies' that are trying to promote products to us? Where is our restraint? Where are our limits and boundaries? Why do we feel the need to be fake on social media? What is really important to us? Does anyone really care what we look like? Can we not cut our own hair? What does it mean to thrive? How can we help in our community? What can we do to prevent world hunger? How can we become more eco-friendly? Is society more important than the individual? What is the point if we're all dead?

We hear about Facebook, Amazon and Google using 'echo chambers' in order to drive our buying style. For most cognitively functioning adults, this isn't quite as subtle as it may appear. We are, through advertising, being drawn into buying sites. Our very brains have become subtly brainwashed; our buying neuro pathways and our feel-good hormones are stimulated. The experience of fast speed shopping also distorts time. In developed countries, we are able to purchase items online in a matter of seconds, which prior to ecommerce would have taken us, on average, two hours. We are able to narrow down our searches to obtain exactly what we are looking for. These actions stimulate our happy hormones, but the reward is short-term.

Sociologically, more satisfaction has been found by engaging with others and strengthening our social connections. Young people need to be protected from marketing and social media pressure as they are more vulnerable and more easily exploited, unconsciously. There is also peer pressure to keep up with the current fashions, in terms of looks, clothes and technology.

The varying governments, senates and world leaders have their responsibility, on whom individuals can apply pressure, but what can we do ourselves, on a local level?

Is it smart to live in a big house? Is it smart to have perfect nails? Is it essential to have a powerful car? Is excess red meat essential? Is it okay to turn our back on the starving? Is it okay to purchase new furniture? Is it okay to keep buying more clothes? Is it okay to want perfect eyebrows? Is it okay to have lip fillers? Is it okay to take rockets into space? Is it okay to worry about trivia? Is it okay to worry what our friends think of us? Do we really need to worry about marriage and divorce? Do we really need to buy so much produce in our weekly food shop? Do we really need to wear make-up? Do we really need more wood? Do we really need more children? Do we really need more plastic in our lives? Do we really need to eat so much? Do our children really need more clothes? These are some of the crazy questions we need to ask ourselves every day!

If I spent less money on the things that I don't really need, what would this look like? We need to buy, think and do things differently. Spend less on rubbish and exercise more cognitive control. What do we *really* need? Can we eat less and upcycle clothes and furniture? Where is your *stuff* made? Eating less not only creates less methane gas, it also lessens potential illnesses (especially where excess red meat is concerned) and the amount of time we spend in hospital, using up more precious resources.

Obesity has no place in a dying world. Only a minority of people are overweight due to an underlying health condition; for the most part, people who are overweight could simply have more self-discipline and eat less. This would in itself have a positive impact on the planet. Eradicating obesity and morbid obesity should be the primary goal within healthcare. If people are overweight, they should be monitored closely and report via their Fitbit, or similar devices, to their doctor, nurse or healthcare practitioner. In our attempt to become 'politically correct', as a developed human race, we have sometimes stopped pointing out where change *needs* to happen. A society which *accepts* anything for fear of reprisal is not a well-functioning society. Offering priority Covid-19 vaccinations to the morbidly obese, in favour of a 'fit person', sends out a skewed message to our modern, developed society. The re-organisation of health care, due to the shrinkage of a widely available workforce, offers reasoning to work in new ways. Prevention is better than cure and with this is the parallels on homelife, education in schools, appropriate marketing / taxing of sugar, fat meat & alcohol and ways in which we can de-activate our negated genes, with a propensity to illness.

Furthermore, we don't need to dash out in motor vehicles every time we think a new task needs attending to. We could incorporate many jobs into one journey. We could give away rather than throw away. We don't *need* Canadian cedar when pine can do the job. We must become more reflective, creative and responsible in our outlook. Regarding gifts, maybe consider purchasing an eco-gift, such as a National Trust card, an e-bike, or a 'Surfers Against Sewage' membership? You can also strive to buy gifts locally wherever possible. Also perhaps opt to stop sending Christmas cards. Ultimately, it is about how we value the right things and people. How we value the right jobs, not just the well-paid jobs. The list is endless. Now, consider the following daily rituals. If you spent less money on 'things' you don't really need...

Could you walk around in old clothes?
Could you spend more money on plant-based food?
Could you install insulation in your loft?
Could you install air source heating?
Could you use tap water instead of bottled water?
Could you barter for goods with friends?
Could you stop worrying about trivia?
Could you ride your bike rather than always driving your car?
Could you work from home more?
Could you join a local committee?
Could you complete a local beach clean?

Checklist

1) Turn it off
2) Invest in eco-friendly technology
3) Switch to renewables
4) Eat less meat
5) Don't waste food (buy / eat less)
6) Compost
7) Recycle
8) Cut out plastic

Eco-practice

Eco-practice involves conserving water, driving less, walking more, consuming less energy, buying recycled goods, eating locally, growing our own vegetables (if possible), creating less waste and planting more trees.

Here are some other suggestions:

- Hang laundry out to dry
- Use more public transport
- Consider becoming vegan or vegetarian on certain days of the week
- Use both sides of the writing paper
- Go paperless
- Donate unused items
- Use long-lasting light bulbs
- Use green cleaning re-fill products
- Use reusable coffee cups
- Use eco-laundry detergent
- Only buy what you need
- Fix rather than replace
- Return gardens to nature

Social media and the internet have completely changed the way we think, feel and act. It is a subtle but pervasive transformation. Effective measures should be put into place, at the local and media / company level, to protect individuals and the planet from the catastrophic effects of consumerism.

I talk of constraint because social media and buying has completely altered how we think and act. My 12-year-old daughter recently said to me, "Mum, please could you buy me a new mirror as the support is loose." In a busy and rushed world, it would be easy to grab my phone, press 'Amazon Prime' and have the problem solved. Instead, I scanned the room and spotted some keys (a substitute screwdriver!). I had it fixed in 10 seconds. Think of the actual processes this saved, not forgetting my daughter, who also had her emotional needs immediately met. In the opinion of Karl Marx, *alienation* occurs when we detach and compartmentalise tasks and living. This example demonstrates that a solution was sought and a sense of achievement reached, through a tiny task. Being more mindful as we go about our daily lives is essential to more effective eco-thinking. How time itself is experienced has also altered. We need to all take a good look at our lives and think about what we are currently doing or not doing.

_____

"Grief spun her heart with the wind, and the rain, and the forest's aching pain. But the moon penned a poem of her resilience."

Angie Welland-Crosby

_____

Similarly to Covid-19 and its subsequent mutations, the real threat for Mother Earth is that it will, inevitably, put us all into survival mode. As this happens, irritation, displacement, transference and projection will occur. This, in short, is where 'people act out', often against each other, when they feel out of control, of themselves and their surroundings. Transference is where subconsciously, someone is responding and feeling in a familiar way, based on their previous experiences and relationships. And projection is where we 'project' these unhealthy emotions and actions onto others. This includes how we subsequently treat other people and the material world around us. The psychological, sociological and social are all unavoidably tangled up. We have already starkly witnessed these social and behavioural shifts starting to happen, more frequently and in a more wide spread way.

It is said that anger is simply sadness which has nowhere to go. Anger can be expressed through criminal damage, emotional outbursts, social undermining, negative thoughts and 'gas lighting'. We shall also see an increase in super empaths. This is where individuals, who have been previously traumatised or sensitised, have an in-depth connection and 'super empathy' with their fellow human beings. Therefore, their empathy levels almost reach fever pitch. Unfortunately (or fortunately), the angry and the empaths often have strong social connections and similarities.

Both ends of the human spectrum, anger and empathy, can be fuelled into distorted thinking or positive action. If you think social norms are skewed at the moment, then they could get a whole lot worse. Children killing children – yes, you heard that right. Covid-19 is just the start, and social media is the fuel. We need to step back and see beyond our thoughts and behaviours. Not to the degree that we damage our own souls and our own boundaries. It just stops us absorbing other people's stresses and trauma. It does not necessarily make the behaviour okay, but it enables us to recognise where the behaviour is coming from. As a society, we will need to become much more reflective, accepting and emotionally connected, if we are to jointly survive.

In terms of social media, many individuals have become slaves to their phones and devices. Social media has completely skewed our neural pathways, and that of our children. It has affected more people than not, so has indeed become an unhealthy social norm. It has distorted what is placed in front of us and therefore how we think. It has replaced 'I think therefore I am' with a subconscious manipulation of the mind. In some areas, we have, subtly or not so subtly, seen a normalisation of hate. Echo chambers is a term used to describe how all (social media) searches, dictated by others, become our own personalised marketing and thinking. This is not totally subliminal, but it is manipulative and widespread. Paradoxically, social media also has the ability to positively connect people. Unfortunately, due to the very nature of the echo chambers, what we are often seeing, as a society, is a polarisation of love one end and hate the other. The part in the middle, indeed the information in the middle, is often left silenced.

In terms of the planet dying, we need to step back and recognise what is required to change our thinking, our behaviour, our communication and our social connections with others. Centrally, in terms of our individual impact, or 'footprint', we can see that we are being manipulated to buy 'stuff', but we still purchase it anyway. All cognitively functioning adults need to take some individual responsibility. A new buzz word for the protection of our planet, is a prerequisite for *restraint*. This is restraint on a consumer, political, local and emotional level. The role of companies such as Apple, could have an enormous impact on what could be positively 'imprinted' into the community and on an individual level.

On a sociological and psychological level, individualism, and indeed capitalism, has out-spun confluency. Individualism has been reinforced into our brains for so long that it has become the norm. Unpinning individualism is the attitude of, 'what's in this for me?' Confluency, through what Gidden's described as the 'confluent relationship', is where each individual is equal and exists in a symmetrical, flowing way. This is the hypothetical world where we are all 'citizens of the world', and humanity and similarity are placed over inequality and social division.

How has this new understanding changed the way we think? How will it change the way we act? It is not just a matter of amend, reduce, reuse and recycle. It is not just about getting on our e-bikes or in our e-cars! It is not just looking to our world leaders and managers to act, review, implement and repeat. It is a completely different, transpersonal and confluent existence, with the potential to permeate not just our actions, but our way of thinking. It is potentially about equality and making peace with Mother Earth. This revised way of thinking, which is social and humane, is individualistic, but not to the degree of placing a burden on others and our planet. It is about moving, historically, from the post-revolution greed dynasty to the degenerate and renewed dynasty.

Individualism has been thrust on us from all sides of the political divide and it is not as mentally rewarding as some of us might think. Confluent relationships describe relationships that are mutually beneficial, sensitive and equal. As material growth rises, so does inequality, discourse and a removal from our sociologistic and social reliability, and roots. As a world, we are indeed staring death in the face. We allow children to die in front of us on the news and have desensitised ourselves to this harsh reality. Our very media reinforces our absence to act and see something as 'elsewhere'.

Now Mother Earth is dying. Do we walk past? Does that make us feel good? No. Reflect, what does actually make you feel good? Is it looking in the mirror or feeling protected and loved? Have you noticed how giving provides more emotional satisfaction than taking? Is our sense of denial so great that we do not care for our fellow human beings? Politicians have perhaps had their day. We are starting to see the demand and social awakening for social and climatic change.

There is a reason why our current perception of happiness is doomed to the history books. We currently, and widely, have a false impression on what happiness actually looks like. James, in his book, *Affluenza* (2007), describes a 'social illness', which is sweeping through the English-speaking world; an obsessive, envious, keeping-up-with-the-Joneses that makes us twice as prone to depression, anxiety and addictions, compared to people in other developed nations. He describes how we are starting to 'infect' the whole world with this 'virulent virus'.

Much more concentration needs to be based on *being* rather than *having*. James assesses "authenticity, vivacity and playfulness" as being more happy-centred (*Affluenza*: page 311). Further terms of reference include the idea, thinking and implementation of hope, future, volunteering, charity and selflessness. An important personal implication of his book is that whatever you're thinking of spending your money on, the central question should be, 'Do I *need* this, or do I *want* it?'

A huge eco-footprint on the planet in developed countries, at the individual and business level, is based around eating too much and, as a result, making ourselves and our children generally unhappy and unwell. There is no excuse for the impact that the over-consumption of meat is having on our planet. Where there are clearly individuals dying in the world from starvation, over-eating has no place in a civilised society. It is very rare for excess weight, at the starting point, to be caused by an underlying health condition. However, poor lifestyle choices can result in underlying genes being activated.

Poverty is no excuse either. Too many people are alleging to be unable to eat healthily but are still walking around in (unethically sourced) Nike trainers. As a society, we have become too familiar with not offending others but I'll say it here: you and your kids should not generally be overweight, there is no excuse for it. There are plenty of support programmes, often funded freely by the NHS, to turn to. These range from individualised advice, through to wellbeing coaches, social prescribing, free admission to slimming groups and referrals to outside agencies or teams.

In Order to consider and / or maintain vegetarianism or veganism, and its related versions, we must also keep an eye on health too. Veganism is big business and is consumer-led. Significantly, some processed 'vegan products' have an extremely high fat content. Also, whilst some are packaged ecologically, some are not. It is important to remain reflective and perhaps aim for products which are less than 4 grammes, in fat, per 100 grammes. Also, thought needs to go into how the products have reached you, in terms of transportation and work force. Thinking holistically about our lives, our health, our emotions, our immediate and wider environment and Mother Earth is intrinsically and avoidably linked.

In a recent survey, children were asked about their aspirations. They listed, in order of preference: being famous, my family and going on holidays. James (Page 506) states, "A government's prime objective should be to achieve the greatest happiness of the people, not the greatest wealth... to counteract this, we need to restate our ideals and be clear that the idea that anyone can do anything is malevolent nonsense, and that, anyway, even if on psychological grounds it were not disastrous, ecologically it is. The solution is not, of course, a return to pre-Neolithic hunter-gathering social forms, nor is it the re-establishment of cloying social orders which deny opportunities to the poor and to women. Rather, it is to create societies which re-define what the meritorious opportunities actually are and emphasise our cooperative, authentic and playful tendencies. And centrally, societies in which citizens devote much less of their time and effort to being superior to one another."

Ellen Henriksen (2018), in her inspirational book, *How to Be Yourself*, describes eloquently how community action overcomes anxiety and increases happiness. It is based around a similar premise of action conquers fear. As individuals become more practiced in community action, they generally see their emotional wellbeing improve. It is not something that happens on a particular day of the year. It is just based around the premise that 'just getting out there' gradually reduces anxiety and fear, and potentially changes you and the world around you. The connection between the person and the community is key. Breaking down these blocks and social divisions provides a new and more emotionally nourishing way of interacting with the world. In place of anxiety is an action of giving yourself to the environment, without excess internal self-dialogue. This involves motivation and people challenging their 'comfort zones'. When people feel anxious or depressed, it may be the last thing they think they want to do, but taking that first step makes a difference. It is about thinking, "I may feel anxious or scared, but I'm going to do it anyway." The Pandemic has made these connections even more difficult and emotionally challenging.

Hendriksen (2018) expands, "The ability to gauge the emotions, beliefs and intentions of others and to respond accordingly is social awareness. Social awareness is necessary and good. It is the closest we come to mind reading. Properly pruned, social awareness yields social pay off. But if social awareness grows wild and unchecked, instead of merely being aware, we get hyperaware. We over-read social situations, think the spotlight shines too brightly on us, and get a little bit paranoid. We take every look and gesture personally. We see threats in every interaction, which makes us duck out or stand silently. In short, it overgrows into capital S Social Anxiety. And there, like the overgrown apple tree, the payoff stops." The Pandemic has, positively and negatively, made us think more acutely about others. The pre-requisition for understanding has become of the upmost importance.

Despite these challenges, it is not difficult to see how accepting how we think and being bright and bold pays dividends. This way of thinking and not always 'following the crowd' is how we embrace the mindset for eco-change. A little bit of insight into social anxiety, bearing in mind that many people view themselves as shy, is no bad thing. To genuinely care about the feelings of others is more likely to make us more eco-friendly, a better friend and a better lover. This is, by default, simply, because we care.

In terms of conversation with others, in our local environment and on the world stage, it is conversation and diplomacy that often achieves a change of principle, thought and action. Ultimately, the goal of conversation is intimacy: it is a word that often has sexual overtones, but it actually comes from the Latin meaning, 'inmost', sharing what is inmost – what you think, do and feel, with others. Moscovitc (2006) puts it this way: if you try to be warm, friendly and curious, then everything else – the blemishes and awkward behaviours – that all of us have, simply because we're human, become much less important to the other person, because we're connecting and building trust with them. This approach, to simply embrace who we are and connect with others, is what makes for an emotionally healthy society. Alongside this stands respect of 'difference' and an intention to hear the voice of others.

This is something that we commonly call 'active listening' and true diplomacy.

As we inevitably see a change in Mother Earth, with more extreme weather conditions and the disappearance of land above sea level, we will undoubtedly see an increase in the super-powered empathetic individuals, known as empaths. These individuals have the power to fully interpret and replicate the emotions, moods and temperaments of others. This is the sub-power of emotional manipulation and a technique of the higher consciousness. It is an energy that happens around us all the time, which modernity serves to hide from us, away from clear light. As people get more in tune with the world around them, a deeper transpersonal state could easily be achieved. The blocking of this energy is potentially where agitation, anger, denial and revolt lie. As discussed earlier, anger is simply sadness with nowhere to go. Denial of our own feelings and the world around us is an unhealthy state in which to live. Dishonesty and delusion can sometimes be distorted by politicians, the news and social media. As we grow as human beings, a demand for honesty and transparency will be central for development. People will no longer be happy to be fobbed off or just base social happiness around money, assets and self-interest. Community and world consciousness will need to prevail if we are to avoid unavoidable global decline.

Each of us lives in our own unique, assumptive world that can be challenged by sudden and disastrous life events. Bereavement (and global change) not only shapes our attachments, but it also turns our assumptive world upside down. Grief resolution, from an assumptive world perspective, depends on the grieving person's ability and willingness to accommodate new assumptions. Indirectly, this may still be affected by attachment style since 'secure adults' can find it easier to embrace change (Wilson:111). From this viewpoint, we can see how it is central to protect children and bring them up in an equal and emotionally nourishing way. Children's feelings need to be emotionally held by the responsible adults around them, if they are to develop into secure adults. Attachment is, by definition, the reliability and acceptance upon the people and society around us. As the world changes, due to climate change, the very premise of attachment and a secure base becomes, in itself, challenged. Our very foundations are likely to become insecure, unless of course we radically make the eco-friendly changes urgently required, at the micro and macro level. Here, we see an over-lap between person-experienced attachment theory and community attachment theory. We have here an issue of world trust as, "Basic assumptions about the world change from; the world is benevolent; the world is meaningful and the self is worthy. After a traumatic event we ask ourselves why it happened. 'Why did it happen to us? What bad thing have we done to make it happen?' We may get angry because of our assumption that bad things should only happen to bad people. If our world suddenly ceases to be benevolent towards us, if it suddenly stops making sense, we are thrown into uncertainty and confusion. We expected our world to be always benevolent and meaningful and expected to feel worthy of living in such a world. A catastrophe that suddenly surrounds us takes away all these assumed certainties of meaning past and present. We only get our equilibrium back once we make sense of our new world and adapt to the changes and challenges it presents."

Tony Robbins, in 'Miracle Morning', further states, "To make profound changes in your life, you need either inspiration or desperation, (Page 11).

In order to gain more insight into ourselves, the following chart, devised by Lindenfield (2000), may be helpful:

Sabotage	Words or thoughts	Inner child wound
Over-compensation	*"I'm going to make sure my children don't have to go through what I went through."*	Often the result of hurt or disappointment.
Over-dependency	*"I'm sure I'm doing it wrong; I'll have to ask Jill or get a new book on the subject."*	Often a result of not having enough approval.
Inappropriate imitation	*"We always did it this way when I was a child."*	Often the result of love being given too conditionally.
Over-protectiveness	*"A person can't be too careful."*	Often the result of insecurity, frightening experiences or being 'smothered' with protection.
Over-ambitiousness	*"Only 'A' grades are good enough."*	Often a result of having under-achieved as a child.
Perfectionism	*"There's no point in trying if I can't do it properly."*	Often the result of not being allowed to make mistakes or take risks.

Sabotage	Words or thoughts	Inner child wound
Over-seriousness	*"Life is hard – the sooner my children learn that lesson, the better."*	Often the result of having had to grow up too quickly.
Irresponsibility	*"Let's have another drink and let fate take care of it tomorrow."*	Often the result of being either over- or under-controlled as a child.
Revenge	*"It won't do them any harm to suffer a bit – we had it a lot tougher than them."*	Often the result of emotional or physical abuse.
Bullying	*"You'll do as I say or else."*	Often a result of having been hurt and deprived of reasonable rights as a child.
Inflexibility	*"You've made your bed, now you have to lie in it."*	Often a result of having to come to terms with apparently unchange-able, negative situations.
Uncontrolled emotions	*"I couldn't stop myself, you made me so angry."*	Often a result of having emotions repressed and not being given advice on how to handle them.

To become sensitised to climate change, we need firstly to better understand ourselves. This insight enables people to reach a higher level of being. From insight, we are better placed to emotionally grow, reach out, help others and become more ecologically minded.

Semrad, (2003) taught us that most human suffering is related to love and loss and that the job of therapists is to help people "acknowledge, experience and bear the reality of life, alongside all its pleasures and heartbreak...the hugest sources of our suffering are the lies in which we tell ourselves." He would urge us to be open and honest with ourselves, about every facet of our experience. He says, "People can never get better without knowing what they know and feeling what they feel." (Pages 26-27).

Furthermore, the neuroscientist, Joseph LeDoux, and his colleagues, have shown that the only way we can consciously access the emotional brain is through self-awareness, that is, by activating the medial prefrontal cortex, the part of the brain which tells us what is going on inside us and thus allows us to feel what we're feeling and learning to befriend what is going on inside ourselves. This is rather like undertaking our own therapy, by gaining insight and being honest and authentic.

As we are bombarded with social media where "7.3 billion people live in the world but you're going to let the opinion of one person stop your good energy" (@mastering the law of attraction), then this level of self-awareness takes discipline, honesty about ourselves and compassion.

What does this have to do with climate change, you may ask? Quite a lot actually! Because we are often consumed with personal survival and just battling against the unresolved anger of ourselves and others. We must learn a way, which for all of us may be different, to manage and filter out all this 'buzz' that lives around us and bites away at the soul and at our personal survival. We do indeed need to repair and survive ourselves if we are to be in a socially aware position to think about the earth. This takes tenacity, reflection, honesty, self-awareness and kindness. We need to remain focused against the modern challenges of our times. We also need to surround ourselves with people who are good for our soul. By connecting as human beings, we are more likely to connect with Mother Earth herself.

In terms of relaxation, learning how to breathe calmly enables us to think about the role that oxygen plays in nourishing our bodies. This oxygen supplies our tissues with the energy to live. Similarly, Mother Earth needs to breathe in fresh air, which is not polluted by bad people and bad energies.

On an individual and trauma level, it is important to receive and feel emotionally safe. This applies not just to women, children and minority groups, but also to men and other groups that continue to be overtly marginalised, such as offenders, travellers, gypsies, the poor and unaccompanied asylum seekers. We are all indeed citizens of the world.

A prerequisite to saving Mother Earth is to work through the relationship we have, as adult men and women, with our own mothers, fathers or carers. Anderson (2018) eloquently captures this extremely well in her book, *Difficult Mothers, Adult Daughters*. On a practical level, she encourages us all to feel and engage, rather than block out difficult feelings. She says,"In response, you may have felt *handicapped* as an adult... by a nagging and pervasive sense of inadequacy or by a cavernous lack of confidence. If so, these feelings have likely been at the source of painful life-long patterns, such as giving your power away, self-abandoning, creating co-dependent relationships, isolating yourself, sabotaging your progress and failing to realise authentic happiness, in life and love." (Page 12).

Acknowledging our own personal biographies and loving ourselves regardless, is probably the bravest thing that any of us will ever need to do. Meaning comes with looking back and we all have the opportunity to either let that meaning either hold us back or support our growth. We must take time to learn from all of our feelings: "Allowing yourself to feel your feelings all the way through is the ultimate act of re-mothering yourself, of holding the space for yourself in a way that, perhaps, your mother couldn't or wouldn't do." (Anderson: 71). By working through our difficult relationships with our parents, we can potentially find inner peace. This also enables us to analyse and reflect on our relationships with other people. Anderson (2018: 71) provides the following helpful questions and ideas, based upon suggestive inner talk:

What are you feeling now?
How do you know that you're feeling it?
Where is this feeling in your body?
What colour is this feeling?
Is this feeling hard or soft?
Is this feeling fast or slow?
What else can you say about how this feels?
How does this feeling make you want to react?
What judgments do you have about this feeling?
Why are you feeling this?
What is the thought or belief that is causing you to have
this feeling?
Think about a time when you believed but your mother (or other)
caused you to have a negative feeling, then write down what she
did or said.
Describe how she made you feel.
Describe why you think she has the power to create your feelings
in this way.
Describe your feeling without the influence of your mother. What
would you be feeling if she hadn't made you feel this way?
What is the thought you are thinking that is causing this feeling?

Make a list of all the emotions you associate with your mother (or father) and your relationships with them, or others. For each one, take the time to summon up the vibration in your body and describe it. Play with it and notice how you can powerfully increase it and decrease it at your own will.

These words and feelings do not express emotion in its entirety, but rather describe thoughts, opinion and interpretation, which once you select them, create feeling. Importantly, they express how you *interpret others*, rather than how you *feel*. This is a crucially important distinction to make because it is here, where you start to reclaim your power, worth, lovability, insight, freedom and resilience. Loving ourselves, nature, our fellow citizens, our communities, our soul, our reason for being here and our fundamental self-worth are all linked – joining together and making change. Letting go of what is holding us back is what sets us free. To enable us to do this, we need to be kind to ourselves, be kind to others and to remain focused. If we all try really hard, this is much more possible than we may think.

"More than anything else, being able to feel safe with other people defines mental health, and safe connections, which are fundamental to meaningful and satisfying lives." (Van Der Kolk: 352).

To move from the individual to the connective level, it is essential that people are focused on protecting, rather than abusing others. This must be embedded at the multi-model (including ethnic, gender and sexuality); educational, social, work, political and world level. This occurs through improved social norms, societal values and reviewing laws and policies.

A key social ability is empathy and respecting differences in how people may feel about things. Relationships are a major focus, including learning to be a good listener and question-asker. This enables the individual to distinguish between what someone says or does and their own reactions and judgements; being assertive rather than angry or passive; and learning the art of co-operation, conflict resolution and negotiating compromise, (Goleman).

In the book, *Emotional Intelligence*, Goleman states, "The fact that the thinking brain grew from the emotional reveals much about the relationship of thought to feeling; there was an emotional brain long before there was a rational one... a special system for emotional memories makes excellent sense in evolution, of course, ensuring that animals would have particularly vivid memories of what threatens or pleases them. But emotional memories can be faulty guides to the present." Here, we can see clearly how the need for insight, kindness and action is essential. As global impact becomes more intense, the very armoury put in place to protect us also threatens to drown us. We are already beginning to see this, firstly in parts of the world already dramatically feeling and experiencing the impact of climate change and secondly, through the impact of the Covid-19 Pandemic and subsequent mutations. By this, I am referring to the relationships between the natural world of climate and disease and the impact this has on fear, anxiety, anticipatory stress, anticipatory events and then subsequently, health, wellbeing, livelihood, fear, anger, displacement, closing inwards, neediness, revolt and confusion and chaos. This full-blown 'neural hijacking' can focus on a perceived or real fear of dying and subsequently it can have an unintended effect, involving emotional displacement, transference and human misunderstanding. This does not mean that people should totally suppress anger, but rather channel it in an appropriate and fair way. As a way of coping with the pandemic and climate change, people have a tendency towards social isolation. The impact of this can result in further stress, ill-health and anticipatory anxiety, or as my daughter calls it, "inflammation of the imagination." In order to keep our minds healthy, we need to find ways in which to social connect. This social connectedness is essential to our individual and joint survival.

Ford (2008) states, "For most of us, it takes something devastating to crack us open, to get us out of our minds and into our hearts. It takes the pain of a broken heart and of shattered dreams to push us beyond the limited realities we have created for ourselves." In terms of climate change, we really need to connect with ourselves, if we are to connect with others and then, the environment around us.

Ford further covers the areas of inner reason versus the voice of fear, shame and selfishness. She describes the inner struggle between the dark and light aspects of our humanity. One voice is relaxed, trusting and stable whilst the other is fearful, nervous and calculating. One holds the promise of serenity, peace of mind and an innate knowledge that things are as they should be, but the other echoes the fragmented uncertainty of the unknown. She describes the healing process for the victim and the victimiser as the same. Through the predator and prey that live within us, we become integrated and emotionally healthy human beings. The wounded ego therefore cannot heal without the insight, understanding and wisdom of the higher self. In these uncertain times, both during the pandemic and climate change, it is not difficult to see links around how uncertainty has a close relationship with emotional wellbeing, anticipatory anxiety and anticipatory loss. At no other time has a degree of trust, resilience and focus been an absolute prerequisite.

Gripped by the fear that somebody is going to expose us, hurt us, take advantage of us, shame us, humiliate us, embarrass us, use us or exploit our weaknesses, we become guarded. Whilst self-protection is important in times of actual danger, constructing thick walls around us sometimes prevents us from being intimate and for asking for help or trusting that we can share our darker thoughts, feelings and impulses with others. And, in our attempt to protect our vulnerability, we potentially disconnect from our vital perspective with ourselves and others, (Hendrikson 2018). It is time to step back and take stock of who and what is important to us. This is, and will be, a prerequisite to the continuation of our human race. As a society, we do not just need to emotionally survive, we need to thrive. For this defines what it is to be human.

The topic of power is important to the re-balance of our planet. Power is to be seen not only in the formal hierarchies, between countries, powerhouses, governments and organisations, but also between those hierarchies themselves, which are crosscut by occupational and professional structures, relationships between professionals and in structures of race and gender. These aspects of power do not simply overlap, they interlock. Unpicking power is probably the biggest challenge to planet earth. It underpins all social and religious structures and institutions. It may even be more emotionally loaded and trauma-inducing than the very concrete underpinnings of capitalism itself.

Central to these discussions is the very essence of where self-esteem is placed, for us and our children. Traditionally, and increasingly during post-modernity, we have, for the most part, taught our children to love themselves. Inner confidence has been placed upon the (modern) societal foundations of self-love, self-knowledge, clear goals and positive thinking. The dichotomy here is firstly, some children in the world do not have the privilege of self-esteem (as defined by modern living) and secondly, these underpinnings are now at serious risk of becoming eroded. It is becoming increasingly difficult for children to have clear goals for the future when they see a future which is potentially so bleak. As human beings, our inner purpose is to better ourselves, develop and prosper. What and how do we respond to a future which is threatened, unsupported and unknown?

How do we begin to stop children feeling angry about the world they live in? How do we gain trust if children do not feel they can rely on their parents or previous generations? Lindenfeld states, "I know that I would much prefer to live in a society where children's *natural* positive outlook on themselves and their lives was not so routinely contaminated by despair and cynicism", (Page 110).

How will we discourage our children from talking to themselves in a negative way? How are we going to reassure our children that we, and they, are confident and in control? How do we point out when our child's predictions are unnecessarily unfair and suggest replacing them with the reality and hope of a more positive outcome? How do we teach them not to undermine their confidence with self-defeating talk?

If this is not going to be a future experience for our children, as adult role models, we need to start working on Mother Earth straightaway. There is no quick solution, but it is essential that world leaders make commitments, plans and reviews. As individuals, we need to demonstrate to our children and other human beings, that we are doing all that we can to be as eco-friendly as possible. Even the poor must make healthy choices and decisions. We are, after all, all in this together. At every level, from social care to housing accommodation, to green spaces, to agriculture, to marketing and social media, they all require urgent review. This is an essential prerequisite to climate change and human progress. If policies and practices continue to follow the present course, the question will be moot. Organised social life will collapse.

Chomsky & Pollin (2020) summarise this global predicament well, "Suppose that sanity prevails and some viable social order remains. Then much depends on its nature. The steps that must be taken to save life on earth from cataclysm may also induce significant changes in the nature of human society and popular consciousness. It could become more humane and just, in the course of the co-operative effort and international solidarity that will be required, to face this impending disaster, in which case the concept of the 'global balance of power' might become obsolete, or at least significantly less brutal in its essence", (Page 135).

———

Mahatma Ghandi wrote, *"In the attitude of silence, the soul finds the path in a clear light, and what is elusive and deceptive resolves itself into crystal clearness."*

So, what can we do to re-visit my eco-list of issues to work on, for the benefit of the environment and to put pressure on others to act? The first step, for me, is echoed in the current words of the Dalai Lama:

"Today I am fortunate to have woken up, I am alive, I have a precious human life, I am not going to waste it. I'm going to use all my energies to develop myself, to expand my heart out to others. I'm going to benefit others as much as I can."

From a sociological perspective, what would a new form of capitalism look like? In terms of market forces, we could see 'work' looking and evolving differently. Moreover, a great deal is underpinned by consumer demand.

There have also been exciting local initiatives demonstrating how fishing areas can be 'fenced' off to harvest regeneration. We have also seen how heating and driving has evolved and what needs to be in place for greener initiatives to develop further. To dramatically reduce the number of carbon-causing shipments we would need to see much less consumer activity. One effect, resulting in a fundamental change and shift in capitalism, may be a drastic reduction in the number of human beings on the planet. With the evolution of new coronavirus mutations and the ongoing, increased rejection to some antibiotics, or a resurgence of 'super superbugs' and avion variants, our place on earth, even with our amazing scientists, is in fragile, real and constant danger.

Sociologically, we could see a 'coming together' of communities and world leaders, but we could also see greater social division, inequality, aggression and further disquiet. As social media fuels our very thinking, which is polarised by echo-chambers and individual searchers, the middle scenario ends, kindness and aggression becomes more exaggerated. The middle, at times, appears quiet. The fundamental changes that are required to improve capitalism will need to be individual *and* community led. We cannot rely on our leaders to do all the work that is required. It is easy to forget that, as individuals, if we act collectively, then we have power too. It is important not to forget that governments, particularly unilateral governments, will give the impression of control in order to maintain social stability and order. Society requires a humane, confluent, calm and non-ego-centric uprising. This will require us to reach a transpersonal level and project our positivity into the communities that we all serve.

The inequality in Covid-19 vaccination frameworks need to be a 'red flag' to us all. If we are to *save all*, we need to *protect all*. The pandemic will be ongoing and has so far demonstrated how we are all intrinsically linked. In the 1980s, the slogan was "Heroin isn't choosy, it will kill anyone." Covid-19, its subsequent mutations, avian flu, super bugs, nuclear threat and climate change potentially pose the same social, economic and health dilemmas. Again, multi-model approaches must be sought and reviews must be undertaken, if we are to take back control of protecting ourselves and our planet. We also need to avoid viewing the world, broken down, as starts, middles and ends. The mutations emerging from Covid-19 are never going to stop. It's essential that we evolve in a new and more honest and equal way.

———————

"That's the thing about pain.
It demands to be felt."

John Green

———————

There are many different viewpoints regarding the interpretation of grief and often, grief is very individual. The subjectivity of grief and the differences in resilience and cultural variation are acknowledged.

Prolonged grief is primarily characterised by an intense longing for, or a persistent preoccupation with, the deceased person. Distinct from depression, prolonged grief is marked by a pervasive yearning for the deceased. Rather like repetitive, back-to-back grief, continued death occurrences throughout the pandemic are likely to have similarities. This may inevitably lead to a significant percentage of the population becoming, consciously or unconsciously, preoccupied with personal loss and global loss. If the effect of global warming is not reversed, then this would potentially induce persistent and relentless feelings of loss too.

Whereas *anticipatory grief* is somewhat paradoxical. Anticipatory grief refers to a feeling of grief occurring *before* an impending loss. However, the 'rules' of life will change, and here is the paradox. We are told to allow ourselves the *feelings* of grief, even before death occurs, to help us 'prepare'. But what if those feelings and the reality are unmanageable? We are taught to educate ourselves about what to expect. But what if, by educating ourselves, we are just preparing for more loss? We are sometimes encouraged to talk to somebody who is also feeling anticipatory grief. This may result in more joint support and grieving and an increase in community grieving. But what if our usual support systems are feeling overwhelmed by loss themselves?

It is often, in these moments of joint recognition and sharing that we find the support that we seek. In sharing our darkest feelings and fears, we discover other people's vulnerabilities, similar to our own, and through that, we can feel fully connected. To be truly human is to genuinely recognise and respect each other's inner personality traits and their individual trajectory. This is the foundation of trust, confluency, connection and belonging. In connecting with people deeply, we potentially find beauty and peace within ourselves.

On a social level, we have already seen the beginnings of a social 'cancellation culture'. What impact does this have on us and our communities? It is more important than ever to support one another, a family member, a friend or a stranger. How is this possible in the digital age? We need to search for connection. We are traditionally encouraged to enlist help and continue with our lives but what if life begins to get harder to live with? We are further encouraged to create moments to enjoy. It may indeed be that we do increasingly cherish moments even more and become increasingly connected. Maybe life will appear more precious, and relationships may become even more important? However, just as easily, it could result in a deterioration of mental wellbeing and an increase in people experiencing different forms of anticipatory anxiety, depressive disorders and psychoses.

Although anticipatory grief does not necessarily make the grieving process any easier, in some cases it can make death seem more natural. It is hard to let our loved ones go. Seeing them when they are weak, failing and tired, makes it, maybe, just a tiny bit easier to (physically) let them go. Emotionally though, the fall out of grief can still be shocking, individual, life-changing, emotional, scary, detached and sometimes, absolutely devastating. How do we find new ways to replace a simple hug? The immense power of touch has been a great basic loss to many during the pandemic.

Paradoxically, Anticipatory grief could also be encompassed within increased anger and displaced aggression, as people try to make sense of why their loved ones (and also Mother Earth) weren't cared for better. The myriad of emotions may come in waves and include anger, detachment, lack of connection, absence, resentment, a new appreciation of what is important or heightened sensitivity. The pandemic and global degeneration also brings to the fore the fact that we will not always be physically present at the time of death. This absence can make anticipatory grief much worse, as individuals potentially experience a rollercoaster of emotions, such as sadness, regret, rage, relief, guilt and despair. This type of anticipatory grief can easily roll into *extended grief*, which is described later on.

Masked grief is where the grief that a person is experiencing is not realised or acknowledged: the individual says they do not have it, or they simply wear a 'normal' mask. This tends to be more common amongst men when, after the initial stages of mourning, they may still be wanting to reach out, but they are in societies, families or cultures in which rules dictate how they should *act or appear* following the loss of someone close. Masked grief, also known as *suppressed grief*, is when you get stuck in the 'denial' stage and simply stuff down your emotions. The griever has become so adept at suppressing their feelings of emotional pain, they take on another symptomology. This denial has been associated with different forms of grief and is something that we frequently encounter in talking with grievers. The grievers rarely call it by this name, but their stories clearly tell us that this is the issue they are dealing with. It is still important to be emotionally present if someone is suffering from masked grief or a particularly difficult loss.

Denial may be used as a way of coping and suppressing what is happening. This may happen at the individual and the country-wide / macro level. The prerequisite for equality is key if we are to avoid global decline. The misuse of power will not stop the planet dying if the powerful serve to protect no one. We are all intrinsically linked, rather like our natural ecosystems.

Secondary loss is an accumulation of all the unexpected ways you may suffer following a particular death. For example, after losing a partner, you start to experience a difference in the way people respond to you, when they're trying to learn how to console you (or not). When we experience death, the grief associated with the loss itself can be excruciating. There are the obvious things we 'expect', although it is hard to describe anything associated with grief as expected. In the immediate moment, the pain of the loss can be all-consuming. But in the weeks and months that follow, there can be a sense that we are losing even more than just the loss of that one individual.

Society frequently refers to death as if it is always one person. This is not surprising, in our individualistic world, but human loss can sometimes be the experience of many losses simultaneously. Such as in the case of a terrorist incident survivor or where an individual who wakes up from Covid-19 discovers that, whilst being intubated in a coma, several of their relatives or friends have died.

Whilst supporting Cruse Bereavement Support on the national helpline, many callers phoned me up simply to discuss the sadness of not having their (non-Covid-19) loss acknowledged. There was a feeling that certain losses were not always given equal recognition. So, even the loss itself becomes a further loss. During the pandemic, I can only talk from my own experience, but I received more non-Covid-19 than Covid-19 related calls. In these cases, the potential for secondary loss to be felt was often even more noticeable. The level or context of grief is never a competition but in my opinion these losses have been particularly difficult. Another difficulty has been around the media statistics of human beings dying as a result of coronavirus. This has sometimes served to de-humanise a death to a number. For each person, out of the 150,000 people that have sadly died from Covid-19 and it's related mutations, to date, there was a person. This de-humanisation can create an environment of both extreme isolated inner pain and potential de-sensitisation. Significantly, any loss is very individual and often complex. Always be kind. And, if you can't be kind, be quiet. This is the only way people can move from despair to respire.

This snowball effect from extended 'losses' stems from the fact that death does not just create a single hole in one's life. Instead, the loss can impact many areas of one's life, creating multiple losses from that 'primary loss'. Although it is easy to think that our grief is solely the grief of losing the person we cared for so deeply, our grief is also the pain of the other losses that become a result of that death. The term 'secondary loss' is not in the sense that their impact is secondary, but rather that they are a secondary result of the primary cause. Understanding the possibility of experiencing grief from these secondary losses can help build self-awareness in order to identify and understand the complex- ities of our own grief. Once we have identified these losses, we are better equipped to face and mourn them. We begin to under- stand that the whole process of grief is comprised of many parts, including the primary loss and the secondary losses.

So, what are secondary losses? As with so many things about grief, I cannot tell you what secondary losses you may experi- ence. These losses are all unique to our own relationship with the person we have lost, their personality, our life situation and our other relationships. It will often be greatly influenced by our families and our role within our families. In any event, we can all acknowledge how some common secondary losses do occur as part of our personal grief experience.

The easiest to identify are often the loss of concrete things. Some of the more common, tangible losses might be: loss of income, loss of a job role, loss of a home, loss of a business, loss of financial security, loss of self-identity, loss of relational identity, loss of a role as caregiver, a new role as a caregiver (at the expense of other things), loss of life purpose (no longer a parent or caregiver), loss of self-confidence, loss of faith or belief in a system, loss of hope for the future, loss of habitat, loss of goals or dreams that involved that person, loss of a sense of a life (or place) shared with another person, or the loss of a future grandchild.

Our support system can also be impacted tremendously by a loss. Death can bring out the best and worst in families, friends and the community. There may be people who are more supportive than you ever imagined and there may be people you assumed would be there for you who are not. This can result in compounded loss and stress. In the event of people being surprisingly supportive, this can be the start of a new and meaningful friendship or relationship.

More examples may include the loss of unsupportive friends, particularly where people become less inclined to use cars; loss of family relationships due to conflict resulting from death and / or money; loss of friends and family of the person who died; loss of community (if you have to relocate as a result of the death); loss from people connected to the person who died; changes in the way you relate to friends, potential loss or confusion of memories and loss associated with giving away the belongings of the deceased. The pain of watching others grieve is also significant, as you can take on the pain of other people's feelings. The most important loss may be the absence of the person and associated anxiety of not having that person by your side. This in itself can affect, or cause partial loss, to self-identity and self-esteem.

Loss of individuals, on a personal level, may also result in us starting to think about the degeneration of planet earth itself. The consideration of our limited time on earth may feel bewildering, unsettling, scary and confusing.

Multi-model feelings, experience and identity around loss has, for some during the pandemic and its subsequent mutations, led to the minimalisation of loss. For a minority, we have witnessed, sometimes as a coping mechanism, desensitisation, denial, insensitivity, indifference, retreat, avoidance, revolt and aggression. This in itself can present as a local and / or macro 'loss' to the community and / or societal values. As individuals sometimes *displace* their feelings, through communication and social media, the very fabric of societal cohesion and functionality is challenged. The loss itself can then become a mishmash of hurt, confusion, sensitivity, anxiety and introspection.

In other areas, we may begin to see less secondary loss more clearly as death becomes more acknowledged and openly discussed. As death becomes less 'hidden' from mainstream society, there is also the opportunity for communities to pull together and provide more practical and emotional support. Friends and family may become closer and more people are, statistically, seeking out increased support from the voluntary and statutory sectors. This mobilisation has even seen some individuals volunteer themselves. What we are witnessing, in developed countries particularly, is a dichotomy between those that reach in or reach out and those that oppress or feel oppressed. These identities and behaviours are often inter-changing and overlapping. The world has undoubtedly become a buzz of community chaos versus order, confluent love and calm.

Cumulative grief may occur when an individual experiences multiple losses, either all at once, or before processing an earlier loss(es). When you have experienced multiple losses within a short time period of time, you may begin to wonder how much more loss you can endure. Grieving multiple losses takes time and can sometimes result in *grief overload*, where you may experience too many significant losses all at once. This type of grief can sometimes be experienced as jumbled up and confused. Time can become distorted and skewed as the brain processes different life events in different ways. The neural pathways of grief can either become too open or shut down entirely. It can be helpful with this type of grief to chronologically write down each individual or community loss, so that the losses can be processed in some form of cognitive order. The pandemic itself, in my view, has also somehow skewed how time, itself, is felt and experienced.

Communities can also pull together in a way which marks a loss(es). Additionally, individuals may find that they are not just dealing with the emotional pain of their most recent loss, but every other loss they have ever experienced as well. Tangled up in these losses can be other types of non-bereavement losses discussed earlier. I would predict that, with global decline, cumulative grief is going to become a lot more common.

As grief overload and related losses grow, there may be an increase in mental health, mental wellbeing and physical health problems. It is important in these difficult times to make an effort to look after our own physical health and wellbeing and the emotional health of those around us. Sometimes, the body works hard to protect itself and puts grief 'on hold' but, long-term, this is not a viable option. Such loss may be felt and displayed in the following ways: despair, longing, decimation, resignation, blocking, indifference, tearfulness, bleakness, anger, irritation, regret, pathological sadness or even madness. The loss of world habitats can be experienced in similar ways too.

Inhibited grief is when someone doesn't outwardly show any obvious signs of grief. Keeping grief overly private can also lead to physical illness and self-imposed isolation. Similarly, *ambiguous* and *disenfranchised grief* is where a bereavement occurs without closure or clear understanding. This kind of loss leaves a person searching for answers, thus complicating and delaying the process of grieving, which often results in unresolved grief. Similarly, *chronic grief* can occur when grief reactions do not subside and last over a long period of time.

The dissimilation of Mother Earth may result in the 'unintended consequences' of increased global poor mental illness and social confusion, competition and potential dissent. Aligned to this is *distorted grief*, which is a complicated form of grief. It manifests in extreme behavioural changes as individuals experience intense feelings of guilt, anger, hostility towards other people and self-destructive behaviours.

Somewhat related, we find *traumatic grief*, which is a condition where (often) children develop significant trauma symptoms related to the death of an attachment figure. When someone dies in a sudden or traumatic situation, our feelings, whether we are an adult or child, can be very strong and frightening. Post-traumatic stress disorder (PTSD) is a condition that can develop following any stressful event. Traumatic loss is comprised of separation distress (yearning, searching, and loneliness) and traumatic or emotional distress (numbness, disbelief, distrust, anger, emptiness and a sense of futility about the future).

Social grief (sometimes known as social death) is where you've 'lost someone' before the physical event. The feelings this evokes can be confusing, unfamiliar and unsettling. It can also be necessary to try and block out the grief as a way of not becoming overwhelmed over a long period of time. This can partly be viewed as a natural defence mechanism of the human brain, in order to keep complex feelings around mortality at bay. Here though, we find a clear contradiction and dichotomy. Significantly, we do not keep mass extinction at bay. Both losses – Covid-19 and climate change – produce social paradoxes. We partly 'block it out' but it is still there. Moreover, the ways we have coped and will cope have become unchangeably altered and have evolved. Hence, it becomes more difficult to move on, look to the future and keep positive. With this comes the increased risk of emotional distress, the unavoidable increase or demand on limited resources and services, potential civil unrest, anger or internalised grief and pain. Understanding 'difficult' behaviours can also challenge the patience of the most experienced practitioners. How we balance behaviours, boundaries and expectations is complex and sometimes contradictory. Sometimes, sticking with 'difficult' people as they try to push the world away, can take experience, insight, *beauty* and tenacity.

Here you can see how the parameters for post-modern medicalised, psychodynamic and cognitive-behavioural treatment no longer easily works. Here are some common 'tips' and advice that I believe will no longer cut the mustard:

Take your time.
The grief journey is different for everyone.
There's no set time frame.
Be kind to yourself.
Don't fear your feelings.
Allow yourself to replay events and find ways to express yourself.
Look to the future.
Time is a great healer.
Try to re-frame the situation.
Picture a nice scene in your head.
Be thankful.
Live in the moment.
Let's make links with your relationships and your past.
Every experience of grief is different.

Here, *collective grief* and *national grief* are also extremely significant. Being sensitive to the grief around us usually serves to prepare us for the time in our own life when we face death or need to work through the loss of someone close to us. Collective grief happens when a community, society, nation or planet *collectively* experience a dramatic or impactful change or loss. Typical to this is sometimes a feeling of embolization, power, powerlessness, or a little bit of both. The middle area between *extreme intuitive grieving* (feeling) and *extreme instrumental grieving* (action) is called *blended grieving*. People who exhibit qualities of both the intuitive grieving style, as well as the instrumental grieving style, are known as *blended grievers*. It is in collective grief that we potentially see again the polarisation of the super empaths and the angry. This is evident, not just at the local level, but also internationally between states, counties and countries. How countries respond to the degeneration of Mother Earth will be critical.

Somewhat related we find *abbreviated (quick) grief*, which can be viewed as a short-lived response to a loss or global experience. This could occur due to someone or something (such as urgent eco-action) immediately filling the void. As death becomes more widespread, this may become unusually prominent, when viewed in comparison to 'modern' euro-centric types (or typology) of grieving. This is in direct response to a new social norm and extreme human decline, in the new world order. What is really required is a response that is more considered and informed, rather than one that is rushed, without foundation or climatically dangerous.

Exploring bereavement theories and applying them to the degeneration of Mother Earth enables us to see the complexities we may be faced with in the near future. These insights should encourage us to understand our fellow human beings better and emotionally *reach out* rather than *close down*. It should also sensitise us to the reality of climate change and the impact it will have upon us all, at the geographically physical level and the human level.

"It is illogical to say, 'I believe in the miracles of science', in terms of what it can do for our bodies, but then say, 'I don't believe in science', when it concerns the Earth."

Mark Sanford

When our children, grandchildren and great grandchildren ask, "What did you do to prevent climate change?" the following responses just won't cut it. "I bought cappuccino-coloured Nike trainers." "I happily used plastic in everything." "Meat was irresistible." "I was busy working to pay for my house." "I didn't think it was my responsibility." "I was busy getting my nails done." "I was so intoxicated I didn't give it a second thought." "I thought Greta was a brand of cheese." "Living in a big house was more important than living in a smaller eco-house." "I needed a new dress more than oxygen itself." "I drove because I needed to see my friends." "I loved travelling abroad as much as possible, too be honest." "I knew that big boats polluted our waters, but I needed my deliveries." "I was fascinated and impressed by space travel." "I turned up the heating to keep my feet warm." "I voted in governments which would make me prosper." "Starving children, not my problem." "Unaccompanied minors, not my problem." "Rising sea levels, not my problem." If all these statements sound wacky and a little bit mad, it's because they truly are! How many of us live our current lives in a way which is actually this bonkers? Such is the institutionalisation of capitalism and our possession culture. We almost do not even think about, let alone re-evaluate or acknowledge, our individual and joint impact on our Mother Earth.

I have explored a wide range of subjects, but the central idea is that we could quite easily see a potential shift and transition from 'survival of the fittest' to 'embracing an eco-community and a world eco / health mindset'. We just need a change of behaviour, a change of focus, a change of decision-making and a change of priority.

At the beginning of the book, I set out some of the key multi-model facts and solutions regarding potential or inevitable global degeneration. I explained exactly what is required on the individual, community, work, national and world level. I also explored how our value systems, inequalities, use of social media 'echo chambers', cultures, economics, our very self-identity, our thinking, thought processes, and even our basic emotions, are balanced on the very precarious foundation of capitalism and wide-spread capitalist, media and individualistic thinking.

The Industrial Revolution and the post-modern era installed a widespread belief in consumerism. I explored how modern societal design and experience is lived out and pulled apart the way in which climate change could potentially threaten all that we currently view and experience, now, as constant. I untangled how our usual world order, in developed countries particularly, could be under threat and the subsequent potential and demand for change.

I embarked on a trauma and bereavement journey, regarding climate change, in order for us all to understand the emotional and confluent transition that is required, in order for us to grasp our emotional, personal, practical and social responsibility for change. I further explored how our very neural pathways will receive information differently and how this will affect our psychological selves and subsequently, how we behave and interact with the people around us.

In re-examining bereavement theories, I demonstrated how the dying away of Mother Earth threatens the very rules under which we think and behave. In the future, entrenched, unresolved, ambivalent and community grief structures could be psychologically and sociologically affected and fundamentally altered. This insight could be the potential change of tide required, which could take us away from global indifference and move towards eco-enlightenment.

In applying this change of mindset to the physical environment around us, we can see how societies may evolve, revolt and / or emotionally join together. People need to reach out and connect with fellow human beings, at the individual, societal and world level. This is essential if we are going to relate to each other; it potentially has the power to heal Mother Earth and stop her gradually fading away into nothingness.

Therefore, to become sensitised to climate change, we firstly need to better understand ourselves. Additionally, we need to educate ourselves as much as possible on climate change and global solutions. This insight will enable people to reach a higher and transpersonal level of being. From a place of insight, we are better placed to emotionally grow, reach out, help others and become more ecologically minded. To do this, we will also need to be supported by governments, who have a global, balanced, holistic, physical, social-earth and people focus.

It is only when we are aligned, equal, transpersonal, community-minded and confluent that we will achieve a deeper, emotional mindset and subsequently commit ourselves wholeheartedly to jointly cure our planet.

Up against the task of saving Mother Earth, we have many challenges; negative individual projection and displacement, greed, denial, self-interest, local and world conflict, poverty, inequality, physical displacement, regional degeneration, indifference, poor infrastructure, continued development, widespread sickness, madness, greed and potentially, war. The development of infrastructure has already begun, and our amazing scientists are evolving even more solid ideas all the time. We generally know what needs to be done but it takes so many layers of hard graft. These multi-model solutions and layers begin with people. It is all too easy to give our power away. We all, within ourselves, have the power, however small or large, to enact and demand change. There have been many times in my life when I have realised that I had so much more power than I realised. Reclaiming how we want our lives to look, and those of our fellow citizens, is what sets us all free.

A new dawn has the ability to awaken us. This will be the time when we realise that our borrowed world, and joint endeavours, *can* and *must* enable us to transition to a new enlightenment. This will result in joined-up, multi-model approaches to save Mother Earth. It is here that we become pure and peaceful. It is here where we will be able to project our healthy, confluent, transpersonal, pure and guilt-free happiness across the planet. Then we will all begin to not just live but *thrive*.

Anderson, Karen (2018) *Difficult Mothers, Adult Daughters*. Mango Publishing Group.

Armstrong, John Michael (2021) *The Future of Energy: The 2021 Guide to Energy Transition*. Energy Technology Publishing.

Attenborough, David (2020) *A Life on our Planet: My Witness Statement and a Vision for the Future*. Ebury Press.

Bowlby, John (1988) *A Secure Base: Clinical applications of Attachment Theory (revisited)*. Psychology Press.

Bueno, Julia (2019) *The Brink of Being: Talking about Miscarriage*. Virago.

Byrne, Rhonda (2006) *The Secret*. Simon & Schuster UK.

Chomsky, Noam & Pollin, Robert (2020) *Climate Crisis and the Global Green New Deal*. Verso.

DailyOM.com, online learning: 'Overcoming Self-Sabotage' and other on-line courses. (2020).

Deans M.D., Emily (2014) *The Gut-Brain Connection, Mental Illness and 'Psychobiotics, Immunology, and the Theory of all Chronic disease*. Psychology Today.

Doka, Kenneth & Martin, Terry (2010) *'Men Don't Cry, Women Do' – Transcending Gender Stereotypes of Grief*. Routledge.

Dunn-Buron, Kari (2007) *A 5 is Against the Law; Social*

Boundaries: Straight Up! – An Honest Guide for Teens and Young Adults. AAC Publishing.

Elrod, Hal (2016) *The Miracle Morning*. Hodder & Stoughton.

Ford, Debbie (2008) *Why Good People do Bad Things; How to Stop Being Your Own Worst Enemy*. Harper One.

Giddens, Anthony (1992) *The Transformation of Intimacy*. Stanford University Press.

Goleman, Daniel (1996) *Emotional Intelligence: Why it can Matter more than IQ*. Bloomsbury Publishing.

Hari, Johann (2018) *Lost Connections*. Bloomsbury Publishing.

Hendriksen, Ellen (2019) *How to be Yourself*. Macmillan.

Hugman, Richard (1991) *Power in Caring Professions*. Palgrave. Macmillan Publishing.

James, Oliver (2007) *Affluenza*. Vermilion.

Katz & Johnson (2016) *When Professionals Weep*. Routledge.

Layne, Linda (2003) *Motherhood Lost*. Routledge & CRC Press.

LeDoux, Joseph (1999) *The Emotional Brain: The Mysterious Underpinnings of Emotional Life*. W&N.

Lindenfield, Gael (2000) *Confident Children: Help Children feel good about Themselves*. HarperCollins.

Marlow, Cayden (2021) *Climate Change Facts*. Toasted Tiger Publishing.

Mental Health (First Aid), England. On-line training / support courses.

Moscovitch, David (2006-2016) Canada Research Chair in Mental Health Research. University of Waterloo, Canada.

Rose, Melvyn (1997) *Transforming Hate to Love*. Routledge.

Semrad, Elvin (2002) *The Art of the Therapist*, Amazon.

References

Van Der Kolk, Bessel (2014) *The Body Keeps the Score: Brain, Mind and Body in the Healing of Trauma*. Penguin Random House.

Walter, Tony (1994) *The Revival of Death*. Routledge.

Walker, Alice (1982) *The Colour Purple*. Harcourt Brace Jovanovich.

Wilson, John (2014) *Supporting People Through Loss and Grief*. Jessica Kingsley Publishers.

Wiseman, Sara *Heal Your Family Karma*. Kindle edition.

Useful U.K. Vegan/ Cruelty Free Suppliers

Naked Refiils

Scoop

Arbonne

Lush

Marks & Spencer

Earth Breeze

Smol

The Little Eco Company

Who Gives a Crap

Josh Wood (hair colour)

Child's Farm

Wilko (own brand)

Ecozone

Earth Conscious

Salt of the Earth

Bull Dog

Dirty Works

Faith in Nature

Knight and Wilson

Charlotte Tilbury

Gosh

Elf

Too Faced

Tarte

Pixi

Barry M

Beauty without Cruelty

Cover FX

Nailberry

Inika

Aesop

Milk

Versed

Biossance

Sukin

Herbivore

Tropic

Action for Elder Abuse 0808 808 8141 (9am-5pm Monday to Friday)

Alcoholics Anonymous 0800 9177 650 help@aamail.org

Angioma Alliance: Because brains should not bleed www.angioma.org

Black Lives Matter blacklivesmatter.com

Brain and Spine Foundation 0808 808 1000

Brake (Bereavement through road traffic accident) 0808 8000 401

British Legion 0808 802 8080 (8am to 8pm, 7 days a week)

Cantonese & Mandarin Bereavement Helpline 0800 0304 236

Cavernoma Alliance UK 01305 213876, hello@cavernoma.org.uk

ChildLine 0800 1111 (24-hour helpline)

Cruse Bereavement Support 0800 808 1677

Gambling Anonymous 0330 094 0322

Greenpeace www.greenpeace.org.uk

Government (UK) g7media@cabinet.gov.uk

Heads Together www.headstogether.org.uk

Headway 0808 800 2244 (9am-5pm, Monday to Friday)

Inquest 020 7263 1111

Jewish Bereavement Counselling Service 0208 951 3881

Jolly Dollies (Helping widows gain friendship) thejollydollies.com

Limbless Association www.limbless-association.org

Love Portreath (CAN) Beach cleans

Marine Conservation Society (Online clothing / other products)

MHFA England Online mental health training support
0203 928 0760 www.mhfaengland.org

MIND 0300 123 3393 (9am-6pm) or text 86463

Mindpanda (A 30-day guide to Mindfulness) available on Amazon

Miscarriage Association 01924 200 799
www.miscarriageassociation.org.uk

Mount Pleasant Eco Park Campsite Porthtowan TR7 8HL www.
mpecopark.co.uk

Muslim Bereavement Support 020 3468 7333

National Centre for Domestic Violence 0207 186 8270 / 0800
970 2070

NSPCC 0808 800 5000 (Monday to Friday 8am-10pm and 9am-
6pm at weekends)

PTSD UK www.ptsduk.org

Rapanuiclothing.com (Clothing and eco-paper)

Respect – Men's Advice Line 0808 8010327

Samaritans 116 123 (24-hour helpline)

Silverline (Bereavement helpline for older people)
0800 470 8090

Spinal Injuries Association www.spinal.co.uk

Surfers Against Sewage www.sas.org.uk

Survivors of Bereavement by Suicide 0300 111 5065

The Compassionate Friends (Death of a child) 0345 123 2304

The Good Grief Trust www.thegoodgrieftrust.org

The Vegan Society membership@vegansociety.com

Urdu & Gujarati Bereavement Helpline 0800 9177 416

Victim Support 0808 168 9111 (24-hour helpline)

WAY (Widowed and Young) Foundation
www.widowedandyoung.org.uk

WWF One Planet Solutions "One Planet Perspective" outlines better choices for managing, using and sharing natural resources within the planet's limitations, to ensure food, water and energy for all 01483 426333

Young Carers 0300 123 1053

"The world is so full of itself. Hearts numb and complacent. It's forgotten how to beat. Ears deaf to the roar of wisdom. Blind to all but the flash. Its rotten core fuelled by opinion. Decency murdered by popularity."
Donna Dawkin

"The climate crisis has already been solved. We already have the facts and solutions. All we have to do is wake up and change."
Greta Thunberg

"You need a change of soul rather than a change of climate."
Seneca the Younger

"We are not alone. Just by the reading of these words, we are tethered together, in a sublime accord of the heart and mind."
Donna Dawkin

"We are the first generation to feel the sting of climate change, and we are the last generation that can do something about it."
Jay Inslee

"If I had only one hour to save the world, I would spend fifty-five minutes defining the problem, and only five minutes finding the solution."
Albert Einstein

"I think therefore I am" (Rene Descartes) (religious enlight-enment) to be replaced with *"We think therefore we exist."* (humanity)

"Shoutout to recognising our own toxic traits and trying our best to unlearn them."
Empaths Empowered @wetheurban

"We both drowned under the waves of words we weren't saying."
Ben Maxfield

"Anyone who believes in indefinite growth on a physically finite planet is either mad or an economist."
Sir David Attenborough

"Sometimes you just need to talk about something, not to get sympathy or help, but just to kill its power by allowing the truth of things to hit the air."
Karen Salmansohn

"But the eyes are blind. You have to look with the heart."
Antoine de Saint-Exupery

"Be an encourager, the world has plenty of critics already."
Dave Willis

"After all this is over, all that will have really mattered is how we treated each other."
Daily Dose of Happy

"Before you speak let your words pass through three gates: is it true? is it necessary? is it kind?"
Unknown

"It takes one action to cause a ripple effect. Be the one to start a positive one so that others can receive it."
Roger Lee

"Words have no power to impress the mind without the exquisite horror of their reality."
Edgar Allen Poe

"A less wild world is a less stable world."
Sir David Attenborough

"A nation that destroys its soils destroys itself. Forests are the lungs of our land, purifying the air and giving fresh strength to our people."
Franklin D. Roosevelt

"Change will not come if we wait for some other person or some other time. We are the ones we've been waiting for, we are the change that we seek."
Barack Obama

"The world will not be destroyed by those who do evil, but by those who watch them without doing anything."
Albert Einstein

"There are no passengers on spaceship earth. We are all crew."
Marshall McLuhan

"It is not in the stars to hold our destiny but in ourselves."
William Shakespeare

"Never has science around the world been so abundant to meet the challenges that we have."
Emmanuel Macron

"To hate is an easy lazy thing but to love takes strength everyone has but not all are willing to practice."
Rupi Kaur

"It was only a sunny smile, and little it cost in the giving, but like morning light it scattered the night and made the day worth living."
F. Scott Fitzgerald

"When the weave of reality starts to fray, and everything false, falls away, all that is left is real, just you, undone, unbound and finding your truth."
Donna Dawkin

"Sometimes all you hear about is the hate, but there is more love in this world than you could possibly imagine."
The Horse and the Boy

"Calm her chaos, but never silence her storm."
K.Towne Jr.

"Softening yourself after having to be tough for so long is not easy."
Unknown

"Today, be an example. Show kindness to unkind people. They may be good people just having a bad day. Forgive people who don't deserve it. They probably do deserve it and are just hurting. Love unconditionally. Your actions reflect who you are. You are a beacon of light."
'Positive Energy'

"The environment is in us, not outside of us. The trees are our lungs, the rivers our bloodstream, and what you do to the environment, ultimately, you do to yourself."
Ian Somerhalder

"Two things in life change you, and you are never the same: love and grief."
Unknown

There is now international scientific consensus on the fact that carbon emissions (alongside other greenhouse gases) are causing climate change. In the 2018 International Panel on Climate Change (IPCC) special report 'Global Warming of 1.5°C', human activities are estimated to have caused approximately 1.0°C of global warming above pre-industrial levels. The IPCC warn that global warming is likely to reach 1.5°C between 2030 and 2052 if it continues to increase at the current rate. The IPCC stress the importance of limiting global warming to a maximum of 1.5°C above pre-industrial levels, beyond which even half a degree will significantly worsen the risks of drought, floods, extreme heat and poverty for hundreds of millions of people.

Cornwall Council

In January 2019, Cornwall Council declared a 'Climate Emergency' in recognition of the need to take urgent action and set an ambitious target for the County to work toward becoming carbon neutral by 2030. In July 2019 Cornwall Council unanimously approved its Climate Action Plan and it is now working on a new Climate Change Development Plan to 'strengthen existing policies, create new ones and make allocations that address the climate change issues affecting Cornwall'.

> **'The Climate Change Emergency affects everyone, and we need to work together to address it...'**
>
> Bob Egerton, Cornwall Council
> Cabinet Member for Culture, Economy and Planning

Portreath Parish Council

In March 2020, Portreath Parish Council unanimously declared a Climate Change Emergency. It agreed to set up a Climate Action Network (Portreath CAN) and to adopt its own Climate Action Plan setting out the actions it can take as a Parish Council.

This document sets out the goals, actions and policies that Portreath Parish Council is committed to in order to reduce its own carbon footprint and to support initiatives in the wider community to help mitigate and adapt to the impact of Climate Change in the Parish.

KEY GOALS FOR THE PARISH COUNCIL
SHORT TERM ACTIONS

To be initiated immediately by the Parish Council:

- [ ] Pledge to support the **target set out by Cornwall Council** in its Climate Change Plan (July 2019) and set a target for the Parish to be net carbon neutral by 2030

- [ ] Use information in the public domain to **benchmark current carbon output**, identify targets for the Parish and track progress against these targets

- [ ] Establish a **Climate Action Network** which will work in the interest of the Parish and allocate a lead Councillor to link with the network and the Parish Council

- [ ] Switch to a **renewable energy supplier** for all Parish Council-run buildings / street lighting etc.

- [ ] Install **LED / low energy bulbs** in all Parish Council-run buildings / street lights

☐ Actively work to **reduce consumption, reduce waste and recycle**. Minimise the amount of printed matter and where this is essential use recycled paper and recycle all waste

☐ Use recycled paper and **environmentally friendly cleaning products** in all Parish Council facilities

☐ **Stop the use of weed killers** and other chemicals in parks, green spaces, verges and paths

☐ Use **public notice boards** to promote awareness and environmental initiatives. For example, 'how to be an eco-friendly visitor', highlighting which establishments offer water refills, safe cycle routes etc.

☐ Commit to using **local suppliers** wherever possible for the supply of goods and services and consider potential carbon emissions not just price when awarding contracts

☐ Commit to **minimising the impact of Parish Councillors' activities** on the environment. E.g. avoid unnecessary travel

☐ **Maximise use of social media platforms** to engage with the community. Accepting that not all parishioners will have access to social media, use printed matter sparingly and target those that will benefit most

☐ Make use of **opportunities to engage** with other Parish Councils, Cornwall Council and national government to promote policies and legislation to combat the impact of climate change. Link with other organisations to share expertise, experience and knowledge

☐ Ensure that **the NDP** supports high standards of energy efficiency and includes renewable energy in residential and commercial buildings. Include provision for clean energy schemes such as Community-led renewable energy projects and electric car charging

MEDIUM AND LONGER-TERM GOALS

The Council has an important role to play in achieving these goals by embedding them in its own policies and actively supporting initiatives designed to meet them. Some of the actions listed below will be outside the direct remit of the Council and will be explored in more detail in the Community Action Plan to be produced over the next 6 months by the Portreath Climate Action Network (Portreath CAN).

Key:

☐ Indicates direct actions for the Parish Council itself

- Indicates examples of actions that could be taken by the community as proposed by Portreath Climate Action Network

POLICY 1. ENGAGING AND ENABLING THE COMMUNITY

The Parish Council will commit to engaging with and supporting the community, empowering it to take the actions required to become carbon neutral by 2030.

The Council will

☐ Develop a Communication and Outreach Strategy to share information with households, businesses and organisations within the Parish

☐ Engage with other parish councils, Cornwall Council and national organisations to promote actions, policies and legislation to combat the impact of climate change, sharing information and experience

☐ Combine resources with other parishes and stakeholders for larger cross community events

☐ Promote initiatives in the newsletter and social media and notice boards

☐ Help promote and support events to raise awareness, educate and upskill

☐ Encourage as many people as possible to calculate their carbon footprint

☐ Engage with the school and other community groups and local stakeholders such as the Portreath Improvements Committee and Love Portreath

☐ Support the actions of the Climate Action Network

POLICY 2. REDUCING CONSUMPTION AND WASTE

The Parish Council will actively support and promote initiatives that seek to reduce the amount of waste sent to landfill from the parish.

The Council will

☐ Continue efforts to reduce its own consumption and waste.

☐ Engage with Cornwall Council to secure strategically placed local recycling facilities

☐ Support the work of the Carbon Action Network in community led initiatives

This may include for example:

- Support the Parish Council in lobbying for recycling points in the parish
- Increasing household recycling rates
- Community composting schemes
- Possible sites for allotments
- Advice sessions – recycling, composting, food growing
- Group visit to recycling / recovery / green waste facilities
- Repair / upcycling / reusing projects
- Plastic free initiatives
- Community beach cleans and litter picking
- Link with SW water and promote water saving
- Community fridge / larder – sharing surplus food

POLICY 3. REDUCING ENERGY DEMAND AND PRODUCING CLEAN ENERGY

The Parish Council will promote initiatives to reduce the use of energy originating from fossil fuels and encourage the generation of 'clean energy' within the parish.

It will

☐ Support planning applications that optimise the use of good environmental design, technology and materials which minimise the carbon cost of the building itself and the lifetime running costs

☐ Support local and national initiatives to increase environmental standards in planning reforms and local plans

☐ Help identify suitable sites for community led renewable energy projects

☐ Consider switching off street lights at night at a safe and appropriate time or install PIR sensors

☐ Support the work of the Carbon Action Network in community led initiatives

For example:

- Encouraging households to check the energy efficiency of their homes

- Promote grants available to improve energy performance of buildings and provide assistance with applications for those that need it. E.g. pop up surgeries

- Develop a programme to facilitate transition to low carbon heating for homes and businesses (eliminate coal and oil dependency in the parish)

- Run DIY demonstration sessions in typically constructed homes to show how they can be made more energy inefficient and reduce the cost of fuel bills. For example, draught proofing windows and doors

- Hire a thermal imaging camera to show heat loss on buildings

- Encourage people to switch to a 100% renewable supplier for electricity and gas if appropriate

- Explore options with potential suppliers for a community rate for renewable power

- Establish a project team to explore the potential for a community-led renewable energy project which would produce energy locally for the benefit of the community

POLICY 4. TRANSFORMING GREEN SPACES

The Parish Council will work to conserve and enhance the natural environment, making space for nature and wildlife through the restoration of valued habitats, biodiversity and green spaces whilst protecting key landscape features.

It will

☐ Consult with contractors and other stakeholders to formulate a plan to manage green spaces, verges and pathways to maximise carbon sequestration and promote biodiversity

☐ Identify potential sites for tree planting, and bird and insect boxes

☐ Stop using weed killers and pesticides on Council owned land and work with stakeholders such as the PIC and Cornwall Council to reduce mowing and encourage rewilding within the Parish. Where possible, making play areas more natural and providing more habitats for wildlife

☐ Monitor, preserve and protect existing natural wildlife habitats, including marine life

☐ Support the work of the Carbon Action Network in community led initiatives

For example:

• Community tree planting scheme in conjunction with Forest for Cornwall initiative

• Encouraging households to eliminate the use of weed killers and pesticides

• Educational workshops to encourage rewilding of gardens, food growing and planting for biodiversity

- Community growing projects

- Keep streams and waterways free flowing and clear of rubbish

- Consider a scheme to deter hard landscaping and replace non-porous surfaces with porous materials

- Establish corridors for wildlife and space for nature for example pocket parks

- Engaging with businesses to encourage them to transform their outdoor spaces

POLICY 5. CHANGING HOW WE MOVE AROUND

The Parish Council will work to help reduce dependency on fossil fuels for travel and improve safety and accessibility of pedestrian and cycle routes.

It will strive to

☐ Encourage the use of public transport and lobby Cornwall Council for improved bus services to and from the parish

☐ Promote the reduction of car use. Encourage car sharing Explore possibility of facilitating a commercial car club

☐ Promote cycling and walking (including walk to school initiatives)

☐ Provide more cycle parking

☐ Improve safety. Slow vehicles down, maintain safe walking and cycling paths and keep road signage clear

☐ Consider weight / size restrictions for heavy goods vehicles travelling through the parish

☐ Lobby for safe road crossings particularly at the school entrance and between the beach and the public conveniences

☐ Provide safe and accessible routes connecting key attractions. For example, from Tregea Park to the beach. Lighthouse Hill to the harbour. Portreath to Redruth

☐ Support the Mining Trail forum in promoting and maintaining routes

☐ Improve signage to, and on, all safe routes

☐ Encourage the use of electric cars. Aspire to all new buildings having sufficient charging points to meet future needs. Consider sites for communal charging points for homes without off road parking, and for visitors

☐ Support the work of the Carbon Action Network in community-led initiatives

POLICY 6. SUPPORT LOCAL BUSINESSES

The Parish Council will encourage the use of local services and products and work closely with local businesses to help them to reduce the environmental impact of their activities.

It will

☐ Undertake to give priority to local suppliers in its own procurement process

☐ Engage with the parish businesses, including the farming community and encourage them to reduce their carbon footprints

☐ Encourage plastic free, water refill and other carbon reduction initiatives and promote businesses that achieve these

☐ Support initiatives to welcome visitors such as information points and signage and promote environmentally responsible behaviour

☐ Support a local produce market

☐ Continue to lobby for the best technological infrastructure to support working from home

☐ Support the work of the Carbon Action Network in community-led initiatives

This may include:

- Creation of a 'Green' directory of local businesses and services

- Carbon audits for businesses

- Re-establish a local produce market, buy local initiatives and 'use it or lose it' campaign for local shops and amenities

- Seek 'Plastic Free Portreath' status and promote other recognised initiatives aimed at reducing the impact of businesses on the environment

- System for waste food

- Consider introducing a climate charter / pledges for businesses

- Promote climate specific guide to 'being a good visitor'

- Welcome visitors – information centre / historical tours

POLICY 7. BUILDING A STRONGER, HEALTHIER AND MORE RESILIENT COMMUNITY

The Parish Council recognises that many of the initiatives to tackle the Climate Emergency also reap benefits in terms of health and wellbeing. It will promote and encourage initiatives which help build a stronger and healthier and more resilient community.

It will

☐ Use meetings, social-media, and co-ordinate with the PIC newsletters for space, to acknowledge and promote initiatives and the positive impacts that they have

☐ Allocate council meeting time to review the lessons that can be learnt from the Covid-19 Lockdown and consider how these may influence policies and priorities in the future

☐ Look for opportunities to engage with younger members of the community and understand their needs

☐ Consider making more spaces available for sports and exercise, an outdoor gym for example

☐ Support events that bring the community together

☐ Monitor progress on reducing odour from harbour and support environmentally positive solutions

☐ Support the work of the Carbon Action Network in community-led initiatives

For example:

• Consider post Covid-19 pledges for individuals

• Good Gym – providing exercise whilst helping those less able with tasks they need doing

• Community transport scheme – Helping the more vulnerable to get to essential appointments

• Community Hub – weekly 'drop in' social events

For further information about this document please contact PortreathCAN@gmail.com